AN ALBUM OF THE CIVIL WAR

★☆★☆★★☆★★☆☆

AN ALBUM

OF THE CIVIL WAR

By *William Loren Katz*

Illustrated with Original Prints and Photographs

Franklin Watts, Inc., New York, 1974

All prints and photographs from the
William Loren Katz Picture Collection

Library of Congress Cataloging in Publication Data

Katz, William Loren.
    An album of the Civil War.

  (Picture albums)
  Bibliography: p.
  SUMMARY: A brief presentation of the causes,
events, and aftermath of the four-year war that
divided the nation.
    1. United States–History–Civil War–Juvenile
literature. 2. United States–History–Civil War–
Causes–Juvenile literature. [1. United States–His-
tory–Civil War] I. Title.
E468.K26   973.7   73-11031
ISBN 0-531-01518-1

CONTENTS

★☆★☆★☆☆

AN ALBUM OF
THE CIVIL WAR

★☆★☆★☆★☆★☆★☆☆

A BROTHERS' WAR

★☆★☆★☆★☆★☆★☆★ Only once in history did the United States come apart and fight brother against brother. In 1861 eleven southern states seceded from the Union. There was a president of the United States in Washington, D.C., and a president of the Confederate States of America in Richmond, Virginia. Soon gray-coated armies from the South clashed with blue-coated armies of the North.

In the bitter, bloody four-year war, more than six hundred thousand young Americans died, and countless others returned to their homes wounded. Yet today the arguments that pushed the nation into war still echo in the land.

THE SOUTH

★★☆☆★★★☆   The South has always been one of America's most beautiful regions. Its warm, moist climate provided a long growing season for crops. Enormous fields produced cotton, rice, and tobacco. As an agricultural region, the South had few large cities. Of the seven cities in 1860 with a population of one hundred thousand or more, only one, New Orleans, was in the South.

While the rest of the nation moved toward industrialization, the South remained agricultural. Most of the nine million inhabitants of these southern states lived in the countryside. The vast majority were poor white people who went from job to job trying to make a living. A few lived in huge manor houses that resembled the splendors of ancient Greece or Rome.

Those who lived a life of luxury dominated the government and life of the South. In a grand style, they commanded enough power to dictate to teachers, sheriffs, juries, ministers, Congressmen, and editors.

BLACK BONDAGE

★☆☆★☆★☆★☆★☆★   Power in the South depended on land and slaves. By 1860 there were some three and a half million slaves living and working in the South. Although three hundred thousand whites owned slaves, most of the slaves and land were owned by only about three thousand of the very rich. With this great economic wealth, they controlled politics, education, and much else in the South.

From the European landing in America, slaves had been captured in Africa and brought to labor in the New World. Gradually northern states gave up slavery. But the South increased the number of slaves. The system of slavery meant one person owned another person's labor and controlled his life. Slaves could be bought, raffled off, willed to relatives, or lost at cards. At labor they could be whipped for working too slowly or branded for trying to run away.

The condition of slavery passed on to children born to slaves. A child born to a slave became a slave at birth. At a certain age he would have to work with his parents in the fields. Mother, father, male and female children labored together in the southern fields. Not all slaves worked in farming. Some were skilled mechanics or did household jobs. Generally, these received better food, clothing, and care. They had to look presentable.

From the beginning of their capture in Africa, black men and women resisted slavery. Aboard the slave ships many tried to revolt. Some threw themselves into the Atlantic rather than become slaves in America. On the plantations of the New World this resistance continued. Slaves broke tools, set fires, or tried to poison their masters. Some met secretly to learn how to read and write. This was forbidden in the South. Others met to plan slave rebellions. Many fled their chains — to the woods, the free states of the North, Indian tribes — wherever they thought they might be free.

No matter how others might view slavery, for masters it was necessary for their profits. They forbade anyone to denounce or interfere with it. Angry mobs in the South stood ready to defend slavery by driving out those who attacked it. Northern criticism was also bitterly resented by plantation owners. The masters wanted no interference with the system.

A SOCIETY BUILT FOR TWO

★☆★☆★☆★☆★☆ Southern life was built for two groups, slaves and their masters. However, others did live in the region. Poor whites had too little money to own slaves. Often they were in competition with slaves for decent jobs. Masters trained their slaves to become skilled mechanics, servants, laborers — and then rented them out. Poor whites could not compete with slave labor.

The result for the poor whites was poverty and ignorance. Many left for the frontier lands of the West. Those who remained bitterly resented the slaves for taking their jobs. Poor whites composed the nightly slave patrols that roamed the countryside looking for blacks absent from plantations. Blacks without passes from their masters were often beaten.

Instead of joining with slaves against their masters, poor whites hoped they would become rich enough to own blacks. Meanwhile, they usually blamed the slaves, not slavery, for their own condition. Only a few aided blacks in their escapes from bondage or their rebellions.

A free black population of almost a quarter of a million also lived in the South. Once slaves, they had won their liberty or been freed by their owners for some special service. But in many ways they were no more free than slaves. Laws kept them from owning land or guns, and from meeting together with slaves. Yet they managed to aid their brothers and sisters in bondage. In New Orleans, some prospered and contributed art and inventions to the South.

Because there were poor whites and free blacks, slaveholders worried about their slaves even more. No people ever accepted bondage, and Africans were no exception. Here were two other peoples who might help them fight slavery. That is why slaveholders needed to control both the government and the minds of southern men and women — to make their slavery secure.

THE NORTHERN STATES AND TERRITORIES

★☆★☆★☆★☆ Some twenty-two million people lived in the North. Unlike the South, it was an industrialized region. Its factories hired many laborers and produced clothing for the world from southern cotton. Its railroads carried manufactured goods to the South and the West. Its ships carried products to Europe. Northern factories produced the whips and chains for the slave system and its ships brought the Africans to the United States.

Yet the North had abolished slavery. Its workmen were free to work for whoever would hire them. Employers were also free to fire their workers if they were ill or injured or if there was not enough work. Workers were paid little and unemployment was high.

Poorer than the poorest whites were the nearly two hundred and fifty thousand free blacks. Given the worst jobs and homes, they often could not attend school or church with whites. They could not vote, testify in court against a white, or serve in the militia. Though Northerners had liberated slaves, they did not believe black people were equal to whites. Blacks in the North were not truly free, though a few managed to become educated and successful.

The North was also a region of tiny towns and small farms. Families owned and ran their own farms. Priding themselves on their free labor system, they resented slaveholders for needing blacks to do their work. Since they made money through hard labor, the sturdy farmers of the North thought everyone should. Westerners resented slaveholders using land for slave labor. They wanted neither slavery nor free blacks in the territories of the American frontier.

THE CONSTITUTION CHARTS A COURSE

★☆★☆★☆★☆★☆★☆ From the beginning of the new nation, Americans tried to avoid conflict over slavery. The men who wrote the Declaration of Independence left out a section criticizing slavery and the slave trade. Southern delegates had objected to it. This was the first of many compromises with slaveholders in America.

The Constitution protected slavery in two places. It gave Congress a right to pass a law that would make sure slaves who fled their masters would be returned. It also gave extra votes in Congress to slaveholding regions. This was called the Three-Fifths Compromise since it counted five slaves as three people for voting purposes.

But in two other ways the new nation tried to restrict slavery. The Northwest Ordinance forbade slavery in the five states that would grow out of the Ohio Valley. This meant that slavery could be forbidden in *all* the new territory. The Constitution also gave the slave trade twenty years to wind up its business. Then Congress could outlaw it.

Without new slaves from Africa, or new land to expand to, perhaps slavery might die. Many Americans reasoned that it would.

These slaves above are working on a tobacco plantation
of the colonial era; below, under the watchful eyes of
overseers who ruled their lives, they cultivated sugar
cane. Above right, an African village in the Mozambique
Channel is being attacked in a search for slaves. Starting
in colonial days, the southern labor force largely
consisted of Africans brought to America as slaves.
On the right side of the picture at below right, two crew-
men aboard a slave ship force an African to eat. Africans
were packed into the holds of American and European
ships and brought to the New World. Rather than
face slavery, some tried to revolt and others tried
to starve themselves to death.

Left, a slave is sold at an auction before the Civil War. Above,
these slaves on a levee road just south of New Orleans, La.
are required to show passes signed by whites. Notice the different
attitudes of the slaves. During the Civil War, every southern
effort was made to control the black population.

GANG OF 25 SEA ISLAND
COTTON AND RICE NEGROES,
By LOUIS D. DE SAUSSURE.

On *THURSDAY* the 25th Sept., 1852, at 11 o'clock, A.M., will be sold at RYAN'S MART, in Chalmers Street, in the City of Charleston,

A prime gang of 25 Negroes, accustomed to the culture of Sea Island Cotton and Rice.

CONDITIONS. —One-half Cash, balance by Bond, bearing interest from day of sale, payable in one and two years, to be secured by a mortgage of the negroes and approved personal security. Purchasers to pay for papers.

SLAVERY GROWS
AND DIVIDES

★☆★☆★☆★☆ The invention of the cotton gin in 1793 changed this. It prolonged the life of slavery and made it more profitable than ever. Now it was possible to process cotton more cheaply than before. The price of cotton fabric fell and world demand for it rose. More slaves and more land were needed for cotton.

At the end of 1819 when Missouri wanted to enter the Union, slave-holders made sure it had a constitution that permitted bondage. Congressmen from the North did not want to accept this. Finally, after bitter wrangling, Missouri was accepted as a slave state. But Maine was taken in as a free state. Congress then drew a line of latitude across the United States. Slavery would not be permitted north of that line. Only states south of it could permit slavery. This agreement was known as the Missouri Compromise.

In 1831 two events rocked the relationship between North and South. Early in the year William Lloyd Garrison, a young white editor, began publication of *The Liberator*. It denounced slavery and called slave-owners un-Christian. Then, that summer, a massive slave rebellion shook Virginia. Nat Turner led a band of slaves on a rampage that took fifty-seven white lives. His daring strike for freedom was finally crushed and Turner was captured and executed. Some Southerners insisted that Northerners such as Garrison were responsible for stirring up their slaves.

The next year tempers flared anew. South Carolina objected strongly to a high tariff, or tax, passed by Congress. Led by Senator John C. Calhoun, the state nullified it, meaning the tariff would not be applied in South Carolina. President Andrew Jackson angrily threatened war, and finally a compromise was worked out. But a southern state had threatened not to obey a law of Congress, and had thought about leaving the Union.

These Africans above were found aboard a slave ship long after the slave trade was banned in 1808. It continued through the Civil War because it was so profit-able. This 1852 notice of an auction of blacks was a common sight in the South.

11

WAR WITH
MEXICO

★☆★☆☆ When war with Mexico broke out in 1846, Northerners and Southerners took differing viewpoints. Slaveholders wanted Texas for new land for slavery. Northerners feared the war had been started just so slaveholders could gain five new states for slavery. Show us the spot on American soil, said Congressman Abraham Lincoln, where American blood was shed. His point was addressed to President Polk who had asked Congress to declare war because Mexicans had shot and killed Americans on "our own soil."

After the war, the vast new area of the Southwest came to the United States. Northern Congressmen tried to pass the Wilmot Proviso. This would exclude slavery from the new territory. Southern Congressmen managed to vote it down each time it came up.

THE NEW
COMPROMISE

★☆★☆★☆★★ In 1850 California applied for admission as a free state. Southerners in Congress immediately objected. There was an equal number of free and slave states. If California became a free state, the slave states would be finally outvoted in Congress. Senator Calhoun argued the southern side and Daniel Webster argued the northern view. Henry Clay and Stephen A. Douglas tried to fashion a compromise that would please both.

California was admitted as a free state. But southern slaveholders won a strong fugitive slave law. Now Federal marshals could enter northern regions and seize blacks they thought were slaves. Anyone who helped a suspected fugitive faced five years in prison. Blacks captured and brought before a judge could not speak in their own defense. Slaveholders had won some important legal points.

However, the new law in practice was very different from the way it was written. Instead of forcing Northerners to help capture runaways,

12

people in the free states battled U.S. marshals and slavecatchers. Courthouses and jails were raided by black and white men trying to help fugitives escape. In Pennsylvania a posse was fired on by blacks and two men were killed. In Boston twenty-two military units had to protect a slavemaster and his slave being returned to the South.

The Compromise of 1850, said one furious southern paper, was "a farce."

UNCLE TOM'S CABIN

★☆★☆★ In 1852, as people were becoming fighting mad about slavery, a book appeared that further inflamed their views. *Uncle Tom's Cabin* was written by Harriet Beecher Stowe, who lived most of her life in Ohio. She had interviewed slaves who escaped across the Ohio River from the South and stayed at her home. Her book was fictional, but told a story of slavery that moved many in the North.

In the South people could be arrested for owning a copy of the novel. Slaveholders were afraid it would undermine belief in their slave system. One black man who had a copy was given ten years in prison. But others, black and white, Southerner and Northerner, read the book.

"BLEEDING KANSAS"

★☆★★☆ The vast territory of Kansas and Nebraska wanted to enter the Union. Again the slavery issue intruded. Should it be made into free or slave states? Senator Stephen A. Douglas proposed having the settlers themselves decide the issue. This was called "Popular Sovereignty." It seemed like a fine idea.

It turned out badly, however. Southerners poured into Kansas, determined to make it a slave state. Settlers from the North arrived to keep Kansas a free state. Bloody clashes occurred. On election day in 1855, five thousand armed Southerners entered Kansas, voted, and left. They had cast more votes than all the people in Kansas.

John Brown first battled in Kansas. His band raided proslavery men and sometimes executed them. "Border Ruffians" constantly crossed into Kansas from Missouri to vote for slavery. Kansas became the scene of a miniature civil war.

The violence also exploded in the U.S. Senate. One day Senator Charles Sumner denounced slaveowners for the violence in Kansas. The next day Preston Brooks, a southern Congressman, walked up to Sumner's desk. Wielding a heavy cane, he brought it down on Sumner's body time after time. Senator Sumner slumped to the floor unconscious. It took him years to recover. In the South Brooks was considered a hero.

The violence in Kansas and in the Senate proved how impossible it was becoming to keep the nation from fighting a civil war.

LINCOLN AND THE REPUBLICANS

★☆☆★☆★☆☆ Out of the Kansas bloodshed came a new party, the Republican party. It advocated a West free of slavery. It also stood for a Homestead Law that would give farms to those moving west. It favored a high tariff so manufacturers in the North could keep their prices high. Slaveholders thought Republicans were abolitionists.

Republicans were not abolitionists. They had no intention of ridding the country of slavery, only of confining it to the South. But for white Southerners, this was too much. Their South was in grave danger, they thought.

The leading Republican was Abraham Lincoln of Illinois. He had grown up on the frontier and always hated slavery. But he wanted to let it live in the South. He would only keep it from spreading to the frontier. The West should provide homes for white farmers, he believed. He did not want slavery or free blacks there.

In the presidential election of 1856 the Republicans nominated John C. Frémont. He lost. In looking around for a stronger candidate for 1860, the Republicans began to watch young Abraham Lincoln.

14

The picture above shows Southerners leading captured antislavery men to their headquarters at Lecompton, Ks. During the 1850s proslavery and antislavery forces battled each other for control of the state government. Below, violence in Kansas: proslavery forces attack the town of Lawrence and burn it during the Civil War.

After being sold in Washington, D.C. and chained together, the slaves above are being led south. Escapes were frequent and reward notices showing a fleeing slave were printed in southern newspapers. This slave at above right has escaped by stealing his master's horse. Others did whatever they could — sewing themselves into sacks, hiding under trains, or masquerading as free blacks.

Vol. III. No. VII.   JULY, 1837.   Whole No. 31.

This picture of a poor fugitive is from one of the stereotype cuts manufactured in this city for the southern market, and used on handbills offering rewards for runaway slaves.

THE RUNAWAY.

Harriet Beecher Stowe (above) wrote Uncle Tom's Cabin *to expose the conditions of slavery. It became a worldwide best seller even in the South where it was banned.*

DRED SCOTT'S
CASE

★☆★ Dred Scott and his family were slaves who traveled with their master to northern and western free states. On this basis Dred Scott sued for his family's liberty. Once in free land, people should be free, he argued. For ten years Scott carried his case from one court to another.

Finally his case reached the Supreme Court. But the nine white judges were against the old slave. No, he and his family could not go free. They did not even have the right to bring a case to court. Only white people had that right.

Slavery could be moved anywhere, the Court ruled. It could not be halted. But Dred Scott and his family were lucky. Their master soon freed them. However, the country and slavery had been locked together by the Supreme Court. Now slavery could not be confined as the Missouri Compromise had tried to do.

The Dred Scott decision came up in the debate between Senator Stephen A. Douglas and Abraham Lincoln. In 1858 Lincoln ran in Illinois against this senator who proposed "Squatter Sovereignty." In their debates Douglas favored the Supreme Court ruling in the Scott case and Lincoln opposed it. Lincoln appealed to those Northerners who did not want slavery in the North or the West. Although Douglas won the election, Lincoln came close to defeating the famous senator. Now, more people than ever had heard of Abraham Lincoln.

JOHN BROWN'S
RAID

★☆★☆ In 1859 John Brown gathered a band of men to attack a government arsenal in Virginia. Their plan was to seize the weapons and then arm the slaves in the area. Brown planned it for a long time with his sons and his black and white followers.

But the raid soon collapsed. U.S. Marines led by Robert E. Lee surrounded the arsenal that held John Brown's band. Some of his men died, including his own sons. Others, who had not fled, were captured. The raid had freed no slaves. It had been poorly planned.

But Brown's daring moved Northerners. John Brown and his followers were tried and found guilty of treason. Calmly they faced the hangman. In his last note Brown warned that only by bloodshed could Americans solve the problem of slavery. He walked quietly to his death but this truth marched on.

John Brown's raid and execution further divided the North and the South. He had provided proof that some whites were determined to emancipate slaves no matter what the cost. Southerners became more fearful that their slavery would be attacked by Yankees.

LINCOLN IS ELECTED PRESIDENT

☆★☆★☆★☆★ In the 1860 presidential election, the Democratic party split over the slavery issue. When its northern section nominated Stephen A. Douglas, its southern half nominated John Breckenridge, a candidate more favorable to white Southerners. The Republicans nominated Abraham Lincoln. A fourth candidate named John Bell also ran.

It was a confusing election. Lincoln's views appealed to many in the North and the West. Douglas and Breckenridge split the Democratic vote. Bell received few votes. Lincoln was elected president of the United States. "Fire-eaters" — meaning militants — said the South must leave the Union. Lincoln would free the slaves, they warned.

Slaveholders who feared the power of the Republicans rose to prominence in the South. They screamed that Lincoln was an abolitionist, and they appealed to southern regionalism. The South must unite and form its own nation, they urged. South Carolina led the movement for secession from the Union.

As seen in the rare photograph of Louisiana slaves above, skin-color ranged from deep black to very white. Right, at Harper's Ferry John Brown led a band of twenty-one men, including his own sons and five blacks, in a desperate and unsuccessful effort to start a civil war by freeing slaves. He was captured, tried, and executed.

CHARLESTON
MERCURY
EXTRA:

Passed unanimously at 1.15 o'clock, P. M. December 20th, 1860.

AN ORDINANCE

To dissolve the Union between the State of South Carolina and other States united with her under the compact entitled " The Constitution of the United States of America."

We, the People of the State of South Carolina, in Convention assembled, do declare and ordain, and it is hereby declared and ordained,

That the Ordinance adopted by us in Convention, on the twenty-third day of May, in the year of our Lord one thousand seven hundred and eighty-eight, whereby the Constitution of the United States of America was ratified, and also, all Acts and parts of Acts of the General Assembly of this State, ratifying amendments of the said Constitution, are hereby repealed; and that the union now subsisting between South Carolina and other States, under the name of "The United States of America," is hereby dissolved.

THE
UNION
IS
DISSOLVED!

South Carolina became the first state to secede from the Union.

SOUTHERN STATES SECEDE

★☆★☆★ Before Lincoln was inaugurated as president, seven southern states had left the Union. They charged that the new president was hostile to the South. They knew that the Republicans now had enough power to pass the laws they wanted. The high tariff and homestead laws could now be passed by Congress. Secession was an effort to avoid these laws as well as an effort to protect slavery.

The vote for secession in the South was not overwhelming. Although people were often afraid to oppose it, many did speak against leaving the Union. In North Carolina, Virginia, and Tennessee, large minorities opposed secession. But there was also enthusiasm as southern states left to form their own government.

In Montgomery, Alabama, the seven southern states met and wrote a new Constitution that protected slavery and justified their secession.

LINCOLN RULES A DIVIDED NATION

★☆★☆★☆★☆★☆★☆ By the time Lincoln was inaugurated as president, he faced a Confederate government. It had a president, Jefferson Davis, and a vice-president, Alexander H. Stephens. It had also seized eleven Federal forts in the South and U.S. military posts in Texas. The new president of the United States could not ignore this grave situation.

Lincoln arrived in Washington without disclosing his plans. He probably did not know what he was going to do. His inaugural speech made clear that he did not intend to interfere with slavery. It also made clear that the country could not dissolve into two nations. He would not start the violence, he declared, but he would meet it if it started against the government.

Lincoln wanted above all else to preserve the Union without bloodshed. His conciliatory approach kept four slave states in the Union.

Maryland, West Virginia, Kentucky, and Missouri believed that Lincoln did not intend to abolish slavery. They remained loyal to the Federal government. Throughout the war Lincoln would try to keep them loyal by proving he would not interfere with the institution of slavery. But four more states were eventually to join the original seven in the Confederacy.

OPPOSING FORCES

★☆★☆★☆★☆★☆★ Next to the South, the North seemed a powerful giant. It had twenty-three states with twenty-two million people. It produced three times as much wealth, had four times as many factories, railroads, and bank deposits. The South's eleven states had nine million people and more than a third of these were slaves. It dared not arm its slaves. It did not have the money for arms nor the factories to produce them.

Secessionists believed they would win anyway. They thought the North would not fight to regain the eleven states. They hoped Great Britain and France, who wanted their cotton, would help the Confederacy. Southerners had a long tradition of military training. Some one hundred eighty–two of their officers had been trained in the U.S. army and many had graduated from West Point.

With slavery, the Southerner lived with violence more than the Northerner did. While the North built schools, the South had armed slave patrols and built jails. Violence was more a southern than a northern tradition. Finally, white Southerners felt their spirit of nationalism and pride would carry them to victory. At the beginning and in most ways, the South was better prepared for war than the North.

FORT SUMTER

★☆★☆★☆★☆ The Federal garrison of Fort Sumter was perched on an island in the harbor of Charleston, South Carolina. Its Union soldiers found their supplies were running low. President Lincoln sent them supplies, but informed South Carolina of this. He wanted to avoid a conflict.

The Confederate forces facing Fort Sumter feared the garrison was being given weapons and ammunition, not food. On April 12, 1861, General P. G. T. Beauregard ordered his big guns to open fire on Fort Sumter before the supplies arrived. The man chosen to fire the first shot was Edmund Ruffin, who had always hated Yankees and defended slavery. He was happy to start the big war.

After thirty-four hours, U.S. Major Anderson surrendered Fort Sumter. The Confederates had won their first victory. The war had begun.

But now President Lincoln had the incident he needed to unify the North. Since the Confederacy had fired first, he aroused the people to the defense of the nation. He called for seventy-five thousand volunteers to suppress the "insurrection." Their enlistment would be for three months. Lincoln expected a short fight. Only whites were to be accepted. But four more slave states joined the Confederacy after Fort Sumter.

THE BATTLE OF BULL RUN

★☆☆☆☆★☆★☆ By July, 1861, Washington politicians and the northern newspapers were demanding a Union march to capture Richmond, the enemy capital, and to end the war. But General Winfield Scott had only thirteen thousand regular troops and needed more time to train his new volunteers. And the pressure for action built up. Scott ordered General McDowell to march against the Confederates at Bull Run, thirty-five miles from Washington on the way to Richmond.

It was a strange battle, like a scene in a play. Announced ahead of time, it attracted the ladies and gentlemen of Washington who traveled to the site to watch. Picnic baskets and bright umbrellas to provide shade from the summer sun dotted the hills overlooking the battlefield. Refreshments were sold and everyone talked excitedly of the fight that might end the war quickly.

The battle proved how wrong they were. Although the Union forces won the initial skirmishes, Confederate reinforcements soon arrived. The Union advances were turned around and untrained blue-coated young men fled back toward Washington. Picnic baskets, umbrellas, and rifles lined the road of this disorderly retreat. A confused and defeated Union army scampered back to Washington, followed by the spectators who had come to watch a great victory.

Washington could have been captured that night. It lay defenseless, its soldiers wandering dazed through the streets. A frightened people expected the worst. But the Confederates did not know how great a victory they had won. They celebrated instead of continuing on to Washington. They also had to learn a few lessons of war.

A WAR AT SEA

★☆★☆★☆★☆☆ After Confederate guns shelled Fort Sumter, President Lincoln ordered a blockade of southern ports. He knew the Confederates needed to bring supplies from Europe and desperately needed to sell their cotton abroad. Rarely did a Confederate vessel manage to slip through the Union blockade.

To aid the blockade, Union naval forces captured some important southern ports. New Orleans fell to the Union early in the war when Admiral David Farragut destroyed the southern fleet and landed troops.

Early in the war the Confederacy covered a ship called the *Merrimac* with iron plates. They fitted it with five guns on each side and sent it off to destroy Union ships. Since all the Union and other Confederate vessels of the time were made of wood, the *Merrimac* blasted every ship out of the water and never suffered any damage. Her iron prow bored holes in any ships her cannons did not sink, while shells bounced off her iron sides.

But the North had also built an iron vessel, the *Monitor*, and fitted it with a revolving turret of guns. In March, 1862, the *Monitor* and *Merrimac* clashed. Iron shells bounced and clanged noisily off both vessels. It was a draw.

But this sea battle proved that the day of wooden ships had come to an end.

President Jefferson and his cabinet (above left) ruled the Confederacy during its four-year history. The Confederate government had a constitution similar to the United States Constitution. The South had few railroads compared to the North. This became crucial during wartime when men and materials had to be moved quickly. Above, Confederate cannons open fire on Fort Sumter. Edmund Ruffin (left) had long hated Yankees and wanted to see a free and independent South. He proudly fired the first shot at Fort Sumter. But in 1865 as the South collapsed and his own slaves fled to freedom, Ruffin fired another shot — this time taking his own life.

Matthew Brady and his photographers travelled with the Union Army in wagons like the one heavily loaded with their equipment. The camera was developed in the early 1800s, and so the Civil War became the first armed conflict in the world to be photographed. Military construction crews like this one above established telegraph lines to link different areas of the battlefield, since communication was so vital during the war. The crew aboard the U.S. Mendota (below at right), a Union battleship, included a number of black seamen. In the famous encounter between the Monitor and the Merrimac (above at right), the real winner was the durability of steel ships.

Left: early in the war, Confederate soldiers and artillery prepare for action near Charleston, S.C.; and a U.S. horse artillery is ready for battle in Virginia. This contemporary drawing above shows the bombardment of Forts Hatteras and Clark by the U.S. Navy. The North ruled the seas during the war, blockading and blasting southern ports.

WEAK GENERALS

★☆★☆★☆★☆★☆★ As war loomed, President Lincoln had offered command of the U.S. army to a respected military officer, Robert E. Lee. But Lee, loyal to his Virginia, became the commanding general of the Confederate army.

Through much of the war Lincoln had great difficulty finding the best officers to command his men. General Winfield Scott, who had commanded troops during the Mexican war, was too old. General McClellan carried on a long series of actions near Washington, moving his troops back and forth to avoid contact with the enemy. McClellan used Allan Pinkerton, head of the U.S. Secret Service, to spy on the enemy. Pinkerton's reports convinced McClellan he was vastly outnumbered, and so he ordered his troops to avoid conflict.

John C. Frémont, a popular explorer and Republican politician, was another officer Lincoln had to contend with. Placed in charge of western Union forces, he infuriated the people of Missouri by seizing land and belongings and freeing slaves of those citizens who had taken up arms against the government. Abolitionists rejoiced, but the border states wondered whether they should join the Confederacy. To avoid this, President Lincoln quickly revoked Frémont's order and then replaced him.

Meanwhile General McClellan continued to hide from battle. He drilled his troops and sent out spies to report on enemy fortifications and strength. But he took no action. A Secret Service agent reported on a Confederate army of one hundred and fifty thousand that turned out to consist of forty-seven thousand men. Once, Lincoln said that if McClellan did not want to use his army, he would like to borrow it. When General McClellan kept sending the White House dispatches from his "headquarters in the saddle," Lincoln thought the problem with McClellan was that he had his headquarters where his hindquarters should be.

Early in the war, President Lincoln meets with his commander-in-chief, General George McClellan. Although repeatedly urged by Lincoln to pursue and defeat the enemy and then march on Richmond, General McClellan was cautious and avoided battle. In 1864 he ran for president against Lincoln, who had finally removed him from command.

SLAVES BECOME
CONTRABAND OF WAR

★☆★☆★☆★☆★☆★★☆ From the beginning of the war, slaves escaped to Union lines. They saw the blue-coats as their friends. But often escapees were turned back to their owners. The Union army had been ordered not to interfere with slavery and this meant returning all slaves to their masters. Some Union generals even promised to defeat slave rebellions in their sections.

But the stream of black men, women, and children to the Union lines did not halt. Entire families rode in wagons "borrowed" from their masters. In the Union camps they helped out, the women serving as cooks and launderers, the men building fortifications. Some soldiers taught black children and adults how to read and write.

In May, 1861, General Ben Butler of the Union forces refused to return three slaves to a Confederate officer. They had been building fortifications for the Confederates, Butler explained. This made the captured slaves "Contraband of War." Along with Confederate cannons, rifles, and ammunition, the Union army would not return so valuable a prize. Slaves became "contraband of war." It was now easier for Union officers to claim slaves as seized enemy property and refuse to return them. Within a few weeks nine hundred contrabands had entered Butler's lines. News of freedom spread fast.

Congress passed Confiscation Laws permitting the Union army to seize enemy property. This permitted the army to hold rather than return black runaways from the South.

SLAVE AID TO
THE UNION CAUSE

★☆★☆★☆★☆★☆★☆ Those slaves who remained with the Union forces helped the army in many ways. Some became nurses and others served as scouts. Since they knew the southern terrain better than Northerners, they guided Union raiding parties.

Some slaves served as spies, bringing valuable information to the U.S. Secret Service. John Scobel, a Mississippi slave, risked his life many times by entering enemy lines to find important information for Allan Pinkerton, chief of the Secret Service.

The most daring and famous slave action took place in May, 1862. Robert Smalls, a slave captain of a Confederate gunboat, the *Planter*, and his slave crew devised a complicated plan. When the Confederate officers left the ship one night, the slaves sailed it out of Charleston harbor. At Fort Sumter, now a Confederate stronghold, they gave the proper signal and sailed on. By morning they reached the Union blockading fleet, and surrendered the *Planter*. "I thought it might be of some use to Uncle Abe," said Smalls.

Northerners found such courage and willingness to help hard to ignore. The war continued on without any end in sight. The North and the South needed reinforcements. The South dared not use its slaves. The slaves in the Union camps asked for a chance to fight their former masters. Why should the North ignore the slaves who wanted to help the Union?

LINCOLN DECIDES ON EMANCIPATION

★☆★☆★☆★☆★ It was a slow and difficult path to freeing slaves for Abraham Lincoln. He had fought the war to save the Union, not to free black people. Even though he hated slavery, he felt as president there was nothing he could or should do about it. Besides, he knew that many in the South and North who favored the Union were opposed to emancipation. And he knew of no constitutional way to liberate slaves.

But there were pressing arguments for emancipation. Slaves worked in the southern fields bringing in crops for the Confederacy. They built Confederate fortifications, served Confederate officers, and aided the enemy in a million little ways. If slaves left the plantations and camps of the enemy, the South would suffer a great manpower loss.

If slaves could work and fight, they could be used by the Union. Both armies needed more men, and here were millions of blacks ready to help.

35

Blacks could fight, build, and aid the Union cause. Their loss to the Confederacy meant a gain for the United States.

There was another important argument for emancipation. European nations were leaning toward aiding the South. After all, the North was not fighting for freedom, but merely to unite the Union again. The fact that the South had been in revolt for more than a year proved its claim to be a separate nation. A bold stroke against slavery would turn European nations from the South. European workers would demand that their governments not help those pledged to continue human bondage. Emancipation would keep Europe from helping the enemy.

But Lincoln was a cautious man. He told his cabinet he planned to liberate the slaves only where masters were still fighting the U.S. army. Emancipation would only be a war measure, he said, directed against those fighting the United States.

Lincoln did not want his emancipation policy to sound desperate. When the Union had scored a military victory, he would announce it publicly. He told his cabinet about it in July, 1862, announced it in September, and did not put it into effect until January, 1863. He was hoping the Confederates would surrender so he would not have to do it. But in the end, he announced the Emancipation Proclamation.

THE RESULTS OF EMANCIPATION

★☆☆★☆★☆★☆★☆★ After the Union victory at Antietam, the President announced his plans to issue the Emancipation Proclamation. On January 1, 1863, it was proclaimed. Blacks throughout the North held meetings to welcome the happy news.

But the news was less than happy. The Emancipation Proclamation freed only those slaves in Confederate control, and rebel guns still held them in bondage. It might have offered freedom to slaves in the border slave states or in land already taken from the Confederacy. But it did not. After all, these areas were now loyal to the Union.

But its message was still one of liberty. As Union armies marched south and took more land from the Confederates, they freed slaves. Saving the Union still came first, but emancipating slaves was now part of the military plan.

Some generals had already moved faster than the cautious president. In three southern states black men in the Union army had already clashed on the battlefield with their former masters. Guns in hand, blacks were fighting for freedom. For them, the Civil War meant more than just saving the Union.

THE UNION'S SECRET ARMY— SLAVES

★☆★☆★ Mrs. Era B. Jones, a southern slave mistress, wrote a friend in 1865, "Adeline, Grace, and Polly have all departed in search of freedom, without bidding any of us an affectionate adieu." Plantation owners were shocked to find the slaves they thought loyal leaving so quickly to join the Union army. "Traitors," many a slaveowner shouted at his fleeing bondsmen and women.

Union soldiers caught behind enemy lines found the slaves invaluable. "To see a black face was to find a true heart," said one soldier. Some escaped from Confederate prisons aided by slaves, and others were helped by slaves in their travel back to Union lines. "The Negroes were fairly jubilant at being able to help genuine Yankees," reported Private John Ransom, an escaped prisoner. He told how slaves guided him through a Confederate camp "actually stepping over the sleeping rebels."

With the approach of Union troops, entire plantations deserted to the newcomers. Harriet Tubman, who liberated slaves during the ten years before the war, led Union raiding parties. During one Union raid she led nine hundred people out of bondage. In her ten years as a conductor for the "underground railroad," she had liberated only a little over three hundred.

In Alexandria, Va., these escaped slaves (below left) are digging trenches and repairing a federal fort. From the beginning of the war slaves fled to the Union lines. These ex-slaves at above left are serving as teamsters with General Butler for the Union Army. This was their first opportunity to work for pay. Slave Robert Smalls, captain of Confederate battleship the Planter *(above), sailed the ship out of Charleston, S.C. with his crew and surrendered it to the Union fleet in 1862. Frederick Douglass (left), the foremost black leader of the day, was a former slave who devoted his life to obtaining freedom for his people. Famous as a writer, editor, and speaker, he argued that freeing blacks was indeed necessary to save the Union. With this in mind, Douglass helped President Lincoln raise troops for the Union Army.*

Above, Lincoln reads his first draft of the Emancipation Proclamation to his cabinet. It did not free all slaves, only those held in Confederate lands. Since there was much opposition to freeing slaves even in the North, the proclamation was issued as a wartime measure to help the Union. The Emancipation Proclamation (right) mentioned the specific areas of the South where slaves were to be freed.

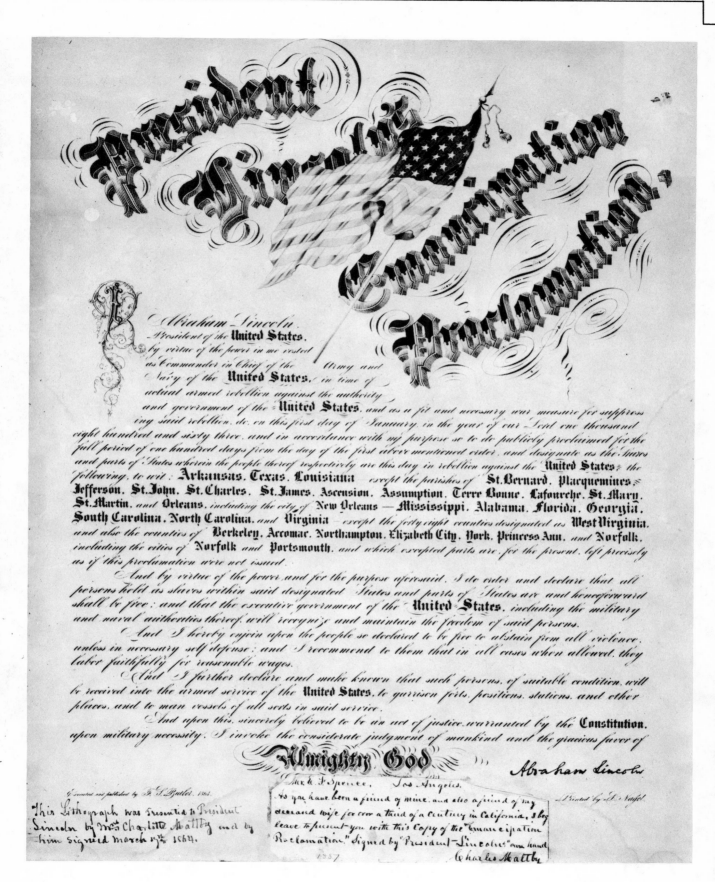

President Emancipation Proclamation

Abraham Lincoln. President of the United States. by virtue of the power in me vested as Commander in Chief of the Army and Navy of the **United States**. in time of actual armed rebellion against the authority and government of the **United States**. and as a fit and necessary war measure for suppressing said rebellion. do. on this first day of January. in the year of our Lord one thousand eight hundred and sixty three. and in accordance with my purpose so to do publicly proclaimed for the full period of one hundred days from the day of the first above mentioned order. and designate as the States and parts of States wherein the people thereof respectively are this day in rebellion against the **United States**. the following. to wit: **Arkansas. Texas. Louisiana** except the parishes of **St. Bernard. Plaquemines. Jefferson. St. John. St. Charles. St. James. Ascension. Assumption. Terre Bonne. Lafourche. St. Mary. St. Martin.** and **Orleans.** including the city of New Orleans — **Mississippi. Alabama. Florida. Georgia. South Carolina. North Carolina.** and **Virginia** — except the forty eight counties designated as **West Virginia.** and also the counties of **Berkeley. Accomac. Northampton. Elizabeth City. York. Princess Ann.** and **Norfolk.** including the cities of **Norfolk** and **Portsmouth.** and which excepted parts are. for the present. left precisely as if this proclamation were not issued.

And by virtue of the power. and for the purpose aforesaid. I do order and declare that all persons held as slaves within said designated States and parts of States are. and henceforward shall be free: and that the executive government of the **United States.** including the military and naval authorities thereof. will recognize and maintain the freedom of said persons.

And I hereby enjoin upon the people so declared to be free to abstain from all violence. unless in necessary self defense: and I recommend to them that in all cases when allowed. they labor faithfully for reasonable wages.

And I further declare and make known that such persons. of suitable condition. will be received into the armed service of the **United States.** to garrison forts. positions. stations. and other places. and to man vessels of all sorts in said service.

And upon this. sincerely believed to be an act of justice. warranted by the **Constitution.** upon military necessity. I invoke the considerate judgment of mankind and the gracious favor of

Almighty God

Abraham Lincoln

Executed and published by F. S. Butler. 1864.

Printed by L. Nagel.

This Lithograph was Presented to President Lincoln by Mrs Charlotte Maltby and by him signed March 17th 1864.

Mrs C. F. Spence. Los Angeles. As you have been a friend of mine. and also a friend of my dear and wife for over a third of a century in California. I beg leave to present you with this Copy of the "Emancipation Proclamation." Signed by President Lincoln's own hand 1857.

Charles Maltby

This photograph (above left) taken in the year before emancipation, shows a group of Union soldiers and slaves standing near U.S. Army headquarters somewhere in the South. Above, this celebration of the Emancipation Proclamation is being held on January 1, 1863 by the South Carolina Volunteers, who were the first regiment of ex-slaves to serve in the Union Army. Their battle-record showed they could defeat their former masters. Below left, blacks and whites gather near a carpenter's shop in Beaufort, S.C. Liberated slaves attempted to build new lives for themselves throughout the South.

Young boys pose for their picture (far right) on a plantation after being liberated by Union soldiers. Their looks show the uncertainty they must have felt about the future. "Union Jim" (above) was one of many ex-slaves to serve as a scout for the Union Army during the war. Harriet Tubman (right) was a runaway slave who made twenty-two trips into the South to help other slaves escape. During the Civil War she helped lead Union raiding parties that rescued hundreds of slaves at a time.

BLACK SOLDIERS

★☆★☆★☆★☆★☆★ Before the war ended in Union victory, more than two hundred thousand black men served in the Union army and navy. Almost forty thousand lost their lives; twenty-two earned the Congressional Medal of Honor, the nation's highest military decoration. In two hundred major engagements they did at least as well as other soldiers, winning praise from friends and foes.

This was an enormous accomplishment. In the beginning neither friend nor foe expected blacks to fight well. President Lincoln thought that armed black soldiers would simply surrender their rifles to the first enemy forces they met. A southern newspaper laughed at the "idea of their doing any serious fighting" against whites.

But the laughter soon stopped with the news from the field of battle. After only one year of observing blacks in the armed forces, Secretary of War Stanton wrote to the president: "At Milliken's Bend, at Port Hudson, Morris Island, and other battlefields, they have proved themselves among the bravest of the brave, performing deeds of daring and shedding their blood with a heroism unsurpassed by soldiers of any other race."

The black soldier labored under the most difficult of conditions. He enlisted for longer than whites but had little chance of becoming an officer. The pay for whites was double that for blacks. Black troops were given the worst weapons and the least training and medical or hospital care. White officers of black troops usually were too prejudiced to appreciate their men's abilities.

Yet the black man's morale in the armed forces was high. He was fighting for freedom. He had friends and relatives to liberate. He thought his courage would win him rights as a free man.

THE DRAFT RIOTS

★☆★☆★☆★☆★☆★☆ In 1863 serious rioting broke out in the northern cities. The law drafting men into the army discriminated in favor of the rich. A person could avoid the draft by paying $300 for someone to take his place. This made it "a rich man's war but a poor man's fight." In New York City underpaid Irish immigrants and others rioted against the law. They were urged on by Copperheads, those in the North who opposed Lincoln.

For four days mobs roamed the streets of New York looting, burning, and clashing with police and troops. Their main victims were abolitionists and local blacks. Black homes were invaded, people murdered, and women and children were not spared. The mob burned the Black Orphan Asylum on 42nd Street, and one child died in the attack.

Order was finally restored in New York by troops brought back from the battlefield at Gettysburg. But other riots had erupted in Detroit and Leavenworth, Kansas. Poor whites resented fighting to free slaves, and blamed blacks rather than slavery for the war. There had always been great competition between blacks and poor whites for the lowest-paid city jobs. The war had merely aggravated that white fear of labor competition. Whites worried about what would happen to their jobs when southern slaves were freed. A mass black exodus to the North would destroy their jobs, they thought.

GETTYSBURG, THE WAR TURNS

★☆★☆★☆★☆★☆ Finally the war on the battlefields turned decisively toward the Union. Ulysses S. Grant was one big reason. A tough, unshaven, drinking man, Grant had been a business failure. In the army he worked at what he knew best. With a wornout cigar hanging out of his mouth and wearing a disheveled uniform, he devised strategies that defeated the enemy. When President Lincoln was warned that Grant was a drinking man, he was reported to have said, "Find out what he's drinking and send it to my other generals."

On July 4, 1863, Grant's troops in the West won a decisive battle at Vicksburg. The Federal government now controlled the Mississippi. This split the Confederacy in two.

A few days later the Confederate army suffered another vital setback. General Lee had ordered his men to invade the North near Gettysburg, Pennsylvania. His ragged army moved ahead hoping to deal the Union a

BATTLE OF
MILLIKEN'S BEND

These soldiers (above left) were part of the approximately 186,000 black men who served in the Union Army. Their casualty rate was far higher than that of other soldiers, largely because they received less training and medical care, and were provided with inferior weapons. At the Battle of Milliken's Bend (below left), black troops battled with Confederates and drove them back. Left, an escaped slave proudly sports his U.S. Army uniform.

Many a new soldier, like this young black (right), sat for his photograph before battle and perhaps mailed it back to his family. Dressed for battle, black soldiers and their white officers (above) stand at attention under the Stars and Stripes near a southern barracks. These rioting scenes at right took place in July of 1863 in New York City. New Yorkers, angry at a draft law that discriminated against the poor, rioted for three days against police, abolitionists and blacks.

Though General Robert E. Lee (seated at far left between two of his officers) disliked slavery, he remained loyal to his home state of Virginia and brilliantly commanded the Confederate Army. Above, General Grant (seated third from left) meets with his staff in this photograph by Matthew Brady. Second from the right is Colonel Eli S. Parker, a Seneca Indian, who Grant, as president, appointed as Commissioner of Indian Affairs. During the seige of Vicksburg in 1863, General Sherman's forces (left) used hand grenades. It was reported that twenty out of twenty-three hand grenades actually exploded and these were enough to drive back the Confederates.

decisive blow. For two days Confederates charged at northern troops. The final thrust was Pickett's charge. In one hour twelve thousand men fell. The Confederate attack was halted.

General Lee apologized to his defeated troops and ordered a retreat. The South had lost around twenty-five thousand and the North approximately twenty-three thousand men — in just three days. But no longer would any Civil War battles be fought in the North. The war would continue for two more years, but in the South.

THE GETTYSBURG ADDRESS

★☆☆☆★★ Since so many young men died during the battle of Gettysburg, it was decided to make the battlefield into a cemetery. A leading orator of the day, Edward Everett, spoke for several hours. President Lincoln had been invited to address the ceremony.

The president delivered one of the greatest speeches in history — a speech he composed from notes scribbled on the back of an envelope. We must resolve, he said, that this nation "shall have a new birth of freedom — and that government of the people, by the people, for the people, shall not perish from the earth."

Lincoln thought the world would not recall the words he uttered that day. He was wrong. His short speech lives today as one of the most significant statements of democracy. By contrast no one even asks what orator Edward Everett said that day.

GRANT TAKES CHARGE: A NEW STRATEGY

★☆★☆★☆★☆★★☆ Before Grant became commanding general of the Union army in 1864, Union generals had concentrated on preserving their armies, exaggerating the numbers and skill of the enemy and talking about capturing Richmond. The result was little action and less daring.

Grant took a different view. The Union did not need to capture the Confederate capital, but to destroy its army. Lee's soldiers, not Jefferson Davis's White House, were his objective. He sent a dashing cavalry officer, General Philip Sheridan, to burn farms in the Shenandoah Valley. He dispatched General William Tecumseh Sherman to cut through the heart of the Confederacy to the Georgia sea coast. Sherman intended to make "Georgia howl!" and he did.

In Grant and Sherman the Union had men who knew that "war is Hell." They acted to destroy the basis of enemy support — railroads, crops, supplies. Neither was afraid of General Lee, no matter how much they respected his military abilities. He was not invincible. The North had more men and guns than the South. And more arrived each day. Thousands of Irish and German immigrants poured into the Union army. Each day the Confederates were running out of men and resources.

If Grant's troops were now seasoned fighters, his generals still were not. They often waited long enough to allow the enemy to fortify a city before attacking it. They permitted an enemy army defeated in battle to retreat without being captured. One general simply got drunk and fell asleep instead of leading his men to capture Petersburg, Virginia.

TROUBLE ON THE SOUTHERN HOME FRONT

★☆★☆★☆★☆ Throughout the war the southern home front was a scene of suffering greater than that on the northern home front. There were few southern factories to turn out clothing, shoes, arms, and ammunition. People went without clean or decent clothing, and some starved to death in cities under attack. The food supply was usually low and often sent first to the army. There was no coffee in the Confederacy.

The government had its difficulties. President Jefferson Davis was accused by his generals of interfering with their war effort. With shortages of food and basic supplies, prices rose. The government had no gold to back up its currency. People in the Confederacy knew the money they used was worthless. Southern morale began to sink.

The Draft Law of the Confederacy worked against the poor. It allowed an overseer or owner of twenty slaves to remain at home. For Southerners the war was a "poor man's fight." Though there were no riots in the South, as in the North, many Southerners avoided the law or disobeyed it.

Morale in the Confederate army began at high level. Many felt they were fighting for a new and glorious nation. But with defeats, the drop in supplies, and a long war dragging on, desertions mounted. Men roamed the countryside looting and killing. Others merely tried to get home to their families.

ARMY CAMPS

★☆★☆★☆★☆ Life for Johnny Reb and Billy Yank was filled more with fear and dreariness than excitement and glory. Neither army outfitted its soldiers in a standard uniform. As the war went on, those men with uniforms could not get replacements for torn clothing.

The Confederate army had a greater problem keeping its troops supplied and clad. Lacking railroads and factories, the South depended on women who sewed for the soldiers and sometimes delivered garments in person. The photographs of the time — the Civil War was the first war to be fully photographed — show crude tents or makeshift wooden barracks that crowded men together. Poor sanitation and medical care kept the camp death rate higher than that of the battlefield. In addition many men deserted, some to join the Union army and others to join loved ones back home.

The northern soldier fared slightly better. At least he fought for an industrialized nation with most of the country's railroad tracks. But his camps too were filthy, his rations and food hardly appetizing. There was little fresh meat or fresh vegetables — mostly hard crackers (called hardtack) and coffee and salt pork. Poor shelter left men exposed to the weather. Diseases were rampant in the camps.

Makeshift hospitals for the wounded and ill were often close to graveyards. And with good reason. Doctors operated with dirty hands and instruments, spreading infection as they went. Anesthetics were in short supply. Most men, particularly in the Confederate army, faced operations with only a shot of whiskey to dull the agony. Nurses were recruited from the countryside. Finally, protesting mothers and wives led to improvements in medical conditions.

PRISON CAMPS

★☆★☆★☆★☆★ The prisons that housed those captured in battle were a national disgrace. The Confederate prison of Andersonville in Georgia was notorious for its high death rate. It provided no shelter and little food. A small stream was all that existed for drinking and washing. Yet it held as many as thirty-three thousand Union prisoners. No wonder that in one six-month period almost fourteen thousand men died.

Conditions facing black Union soldiers were even worse. Their camps were given less medical aid and supplies. The men had to make up for poor conditions through their own labor. Female ex-slaves served as nurses, and in some instances taught the men how to read. Susie King Taylor, an ex-slave for a South Carolina black regiment, later wrote a book about the work and the heroism of the men.

Some black soldiers captured in battle never reached prison. After the Confederacy ordered the death of blacks captured in the Union uniform, there were murders of black prisoners. When black troops at Fort Pillow surrendered in 1864, they were massacred by Confederates. Men were shot in cold blood or locked in wooden cabins that were set afire.

This barbaric practice was halted when President Lincoln announced that the North would kill Confederate prisoners if the South did not halt the murders.

The Battle of Gettysburg (above) was a decisive victory for the Union Army. A German regiment, the Steuben Volunteers (below), lines up in New York City before sailing south in May, 1861. Thousands of immigrants served in the Union Army.

These southern railroad tracks (above) are being twisted into "bow-ties" by Sherman's army. Below, the Wilson Zouaves regiment — more Union manpower consisting of nearly 1200 men recruited by Colonel Wilson (center) from New York City's criminal classes.

At this encampment of southern refugees (above left) who fled from Vicksburg, Miss. in 1863, a group of women tries to establish a normal way of life in the woods. The Confederate government issued its own paper money (left) to finance the South's war effort. Because its economic position was poor, this money was soon considered almost worthless. This picture (above) of two black soldiers in Confederate uniform as seen through a field glass was published in Harper's Weekly. Actually, blacks were never armed by their former masters, although many were used as servants to southern officers.

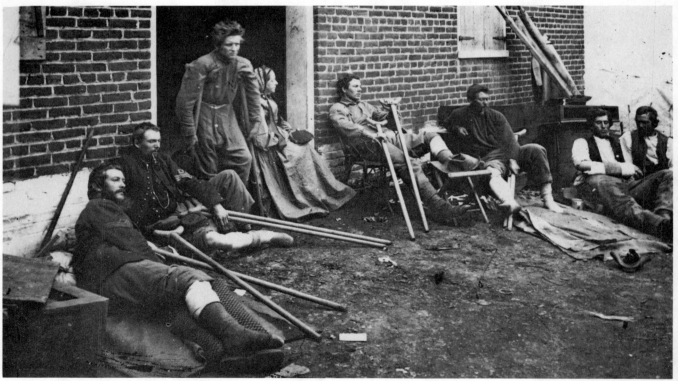

A major problem during the Civil War was caring for the wounded (above). Desperately needed medical supplies and properly trained surgeons were rarely available, particularly in the South. These wounded soldiers at Fredericksburg, Va. in 1864 (below), were just a few of the thousands of young men who had been hurt in the Civil War.

Above, Union soldiers pass through the kitchen in their army camp near Jefferson City, Mo. Army food was neither substantial nor very tasty. Military discipline was a problem for both sides during the war. The Seventy-ninth New York Regiment (below) was stripped of its colors in 1861 for insubordination and mutiny.

Above left, the infamous Andersonville Prison in the South where thousands of captured Union soldiers died from overcrowding and poor food and water. After the black troops surrendered to the Confederates at Fort Pillow in 1864, they were massacred by their captors (below). The Confederate government announced that it would refuse to treat black soldiers as prisoners of war. Above, President Lincoln with his son, Tad, late in the war.

President Lincoln reads his Second Inaugural Address after defeating the Democratic presidential candidate, George McClellan. Lincoln urged the nation to quickly bind up its wounds and be lenient toward the South.

ELECTION
OF 1864

★☆★☆★ In the middle of the Civil War the United States faced a presidential election. For the first time in history a democracy would have to choose a chief executive during a war that divided the nation. Lincoln was easily renominated by his own party. Andrew Johnson of Tennessee ran for vice-president, largely to prove that Republicans wanted unity in the country. Johnson, although a Southerner, had opposed secession.

But opposition to Lincoln within his own party mounted before election. Some asked why he had not made peace with the Confederates. Some felt he was being too easy on Southerners who sought to destroy the Union. By August the president felt it was "probable that this administration will not be re-elected."

The Democrats nominated General George McClellan, whom Lincoln had had to remove for his failure to fight the enemy. Those favoring southern secession and immediate negotiated peace and opposing emancipation supported the Democrats.

General Sherman, driving hard into the Confederacy, captured Atlanta, Georgia, in September before the election. Talk of negotiated peace and voting down Lincoln began to vanish. More people began to talk of winning the victory over those who had torn the Union apart. Lincoln won a second term as president, defeating McClellan.

SHERMAN CUTS
THE SOUTH
IN HALF

★☆★☆★☆ With Sherman's army marching across the South to the sea, Confederate forces lost heart. "Two thirds of our men are absent . . . most of them absent without leave," President Jefferson Davis admitted. More than a failure of supplies or men, the South was losing the fight to believe it could win. A disheartened army began to crumble.

Sherman's army cut a path sixty miles wide as it pushed toward Savannah, Georgia. A vast army of runaway slaves, larger than his armed forces, followed in the wake of the Yankee general. On the Sea Islands of Georgia and South Carolina, Sherman issued an order giving Confederates' lands to their slaves. The battle for a new South was beginning.

Southern cities were left in ruins, the countryside stripped of food and livestock by Sherman's men. Deserters, escaped slaves, veterans, and outlaws roamed the South, and drove out law and order.

THE WAR'S END

★☆★☆★☆★☆★☆ Two of the Union army's objectives had been realized. The blockade had kept the Confederacy from receiving money or supplies from Europe. Sherman had cut the South in two, preventing effective communication. Now only the capture of Richmond remained. Just one hundred miles from the capital at Washington, it had been impossible to capture throughout the war.

By April, 1865, Lee's fifty-four thousand troops guarding Richmond faced Grant's opposing army of one hundred and fifteen thousand. One effort to turn back the Union forces failed. Instead, General Sheridan turned Lee's right flank at the Battle of Five Forks. The next day General Grant thrust his troops through the center of the enemy line. Within twenty-four hours Grant's army had captured Richmond.

But Grant did not halt and rejoice. He hastened after Lee's retreating men. Sheridan came up behind Lee, closing his route to the west. What was his responsibility to his government and people, General Lee wondered. "But it is our duty to live, for what will become of the women and children of the South, if we are not here to support and protect them."

General Lee ordered a white flag displayed and asked for a meeting with General Grant. At Appomattox Court House the two generals met.

THE SURRENDER

★☆★☆★☆★☆★☆★☆ General Lee, gracious and proud, still carried his jewel-studded sword. His full dress uniform was in marked contrast to Grant's. The Union general wore a private's shirt, unbuttoned, and carried no sword. In defeat they still respected each other.

General Grant sat down and wrote out the terms of the surrender. Only weapons handed out by the Confederate government were to be turned in. Lee's men could take their horses since they would need them for farming. Confederate officers could keep their sidearms. Those with mules could take them home. "This," said General Lee, "will do much to conciliating our people." Then he got on his horse, Traveller, and rode off.

The Union soldiers, hearing that the surrender had been signed, began to cheer. General Grant ordered the cheering stopped. It was wrong, he felt, to cheer for the defeat of one's own countrymen.

DEATH OF A PRESIDENT

★☆★☆★☆★☆ President Lincoln was visiting Richmond when the surrender was written. He returned to Washington and received the news that the great war was over. He had already begun plans for a peace that would bring the nation together again. Not bitterness, but renewed friendship, was his goal. Many in Congress disagreed with his view. They felt the South must be punished for waging war, and the slaves must have their freedom assured.

A few days after the surrender, the president attended a performance of *Our American Cousin* at the Ford Theater. At 10:15 P.M. John Wilkes Booth, an actor who hated Yankees, stepped into the president's box and shot him in the head. Booth then escaped, but was later killed.

Lincoln was carried across the street, where he died the next morning. Standing before the White House in a cold rain were several hundred black people, grieving. What would happen now?

As Sherman's army moved through the South, an army almost as large and composed of ex-slaves followed in their wake (above left). When General Sherman reached the Georgia sea-coast, he issued an order giving ex-slaves land that had been abandoned by former slave owners. Unsuccessful attempts were made to force blacks into the Union Army in 1862 in the South Carolina Sea Islands (below left), which the North captured early in the war. Above, Cary Street in Richmond, Va. shows the devastation of four years of war.

After the capture of Richmond, Va., a group of mostly young blacks (above left) gathers near a canal bank to have their picture taken. Damaged buildings can be seen in the background. Below left, this building in South Carolina became a freedom store after Union troops liberated the slaves. With General Grant standing in the background, General Lee (above) leaves Appomattox for his plantation home in Virginia.

$30,000 REWARD

DESCRIPTION

OF

JOHN WILKES BOOTH !

Who Assassinated the PRESIDENT on the Evening of April 14th, 1865.

Height 5 feet 8 inches; weight 160 pounds; compact built; hair jet black, inclined to curl, medium length, parted behind; eyes black, and heavy dark eye-brows; wears a large seal ring on little finger; when talking inclines his head forward; looks down.

Description of the Person who Attempted to Assassinate Hon. W. H. Seward, Secretary of State.

Height 6 feet 1 inch; hair black, thick, full and straight; no beard, nor appearance of beard; cheeks red on the jaws; face moderately full; 22 or 23 years of age; eyes color not known—large eyes, not prominent; brows not heavy, but dark; face not large, but rather round; complexion healthy; nose straight and well formed, medium size; mouth small; lips thin; upper lip protruded when he talked; chin pointed and prominent; head medium size; neck short, and of medium length; hands soft and small; fingers tapering; shows no signs of hard labor; broad shoulders; taper waist; straight figure; strong-looking man; manner not gentlemanly, but vulgar. Overcoat double-breasted, color mixed of pink and grey spots, small—was a sack overcoat, pockets in side and one on the breast, with lappells or flaps; pants black, common stuff; new heavy boots; voice small and thin, inclined to tenor.

The Common Council of Washington, D. C., have offered a reward of $20,000 for the arrest and conviction of these Assassins, in addition to which I will pay $10,000.

L. C. BAKER,
Colonel and Agent War Department.

This playbill (right) was found in President Lincoln's theater box after his assassination. The reward notice (above) was posted for John Wilkes Booth and circulated by the Secret Service. Far right, the funeral procession for President Abraham Lincoln on Pennsylvania Avenue, Washington, D.C., April 19, 1865.

FORD'S THEATRE

TENTH STREET, ABOVE E.

SEASON II ....WEEK XXXI .... NIGHT 196
WHOLE NUMBER OF NIGHTS, 495.

JOHN T. FORD .... PROPRIETOR AND MANAGER
(Also of Holliday St. Theatre, Baltimore, and Academy of Music, Phil'a.)
Stage Manager.. J. B. WRIGHT
Treasurer.. H. CLAY FORD

Friday Evening, April 14th, 1865

BENEFIT !

—AND—

LAST NIGHT

OF MISS

LAURA KEENE

THE DISTINGUISHED MANAGERESS, AUTHORESS AND ACTRESS,
Supported by

MR. JOHN DYOTT

AND

MR. HARRY HAWK.

TOM TAYLOR'S CELEBRATED ECCENTRIC COMEDY,
As originally produced in America by Miss Keene, and performed by her upwards of

ONE THOUSAND NIGHTS,

ENTITLED

OUR AMERICAN

COUSIN

FLORENCE TRENCHARD.............. MISS LAURA KEENE
(Her original character.)

Abel Murcott, Clerk to Attorney,...........................John Dyott
Asa Trenchard...Harry Hawk
Sir Edward Trenchard ....T. C. GOURLAY
Lord Dundreary ....E. A. EMERSON
Mr. Coyle, Attorney....................................J. MATTHEWS
Lieutenant Vernon, R. N. ....W. J. FERGUSON
Captain De Boots ....C. BYRNES
Binney ....G. G. SPEAR
Buddicomb, a valet......................................J. H. EVANS
John Whicker, a gardener.............................J. L. DeBONAY
Rasper, a groom...
Bailiffs...........................G. A. PARKHURST and L. JOHNSON
Mary Trenchard..................................Miss J. GOURLAY
Mrs. Mountchessington..............................Mrs. H. MUZZY
Augusta.... .... Miss H. TRUEMAN
Georgiana...Miss M. HART
Sharpe...Mrs. J. H. EVANS
Skillet ....Miss M. GOURLAY

SATURDAY EVENING, APRIL 15,

BENEFIT of Miss JENNIE GOURLAY

When will be presented BOUCICAULT'S Great Sensation Drama,

THE OCTOROON

Easter Monday, April 17, Engagement of the YOUNG AMERICAN TRAGEDIAN,

EDWIN ADAMS

FOR TWELVE NIGHTS ONLY.

THE CIVIL WAR
ON BALANCE

★☆★☆★☆★ Though the Confederacy had better generals and a population better prepared for warfare, the North had won. Its superior manpower, industrialization, banks, and railroads had counted in the long run. During the war eight hundred thousand immigrants had poured into the North and four hundred thousand foreign-born had served in the army and navy. Hungarians, Poles, Italians, and soldiers of many other nationalities had joined the Garibaldi Regiment. There were several regiments of Irish-Americans and German-Americans. More than two hundred thousand black men had served.

The South had no Garibaldi volunteers, no black troops. Its dream of a southern nation proved unworkable. The Union blockade cut it off from European aid. The Confederate government could not raise enough money or produce enough materials of war, and its dreams died on the battlefield waiting for reserves that never came. It dared not arm its slaves. Its dream of a separate nation was drowned in blood.

The Civil War restored the United States of America and proved that no portion could ever leave the Union. It also ended slavery. Passage of the 13th Amendment to the U.S. Constitution in 1865 made emancipation permanent. Though slavery had vanished, white fear and hate of blacks remained. Both sides had sent armies into battle that believed in white supremacy. Slavery had died that the Union might live.

But Americans on both sides had given themselves an opportunity to change racial relationships. They could move from slavery to equality and justice. In binding the nation's wounds, they could cure the cancer spread by slavery. Unfortunately, they would miss this great opportunity.

Left, soldiers are mustered out of the U.S. Army and rejoin their families at Little Rock, Ark. in 1865. Over, this drawing of the Union dead was published in Harper's Weekly at the end of the war. White men and black men had fought and died together to defeat the Confederacy.

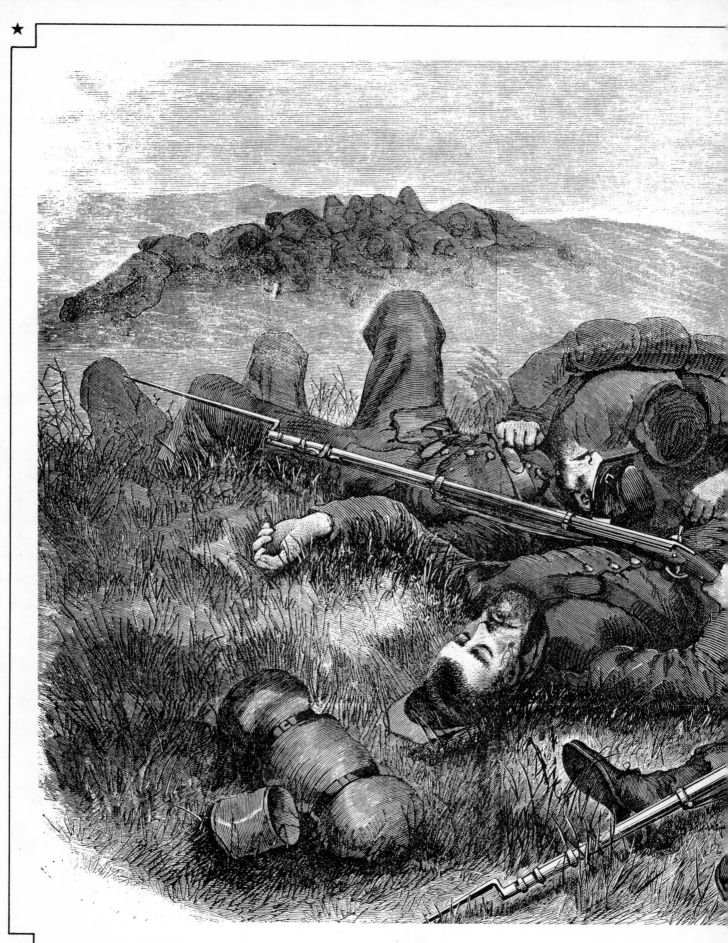

BIBLIOGRAPHY

★☆★☆★☆★☆★☆

Catton, Bruce. *Never Call Retreat*. New York: Pocket Books, 1967.

—— *Terrible Swift Sword*. New York: Pocket Books, 1967.

—— *The Coming Fury*. New York: Pocket Books, 1961.

—— *This Hallowed Ground*. New York: Pocket Books, 1961.

Franklin, John Hope. *The Emancipation Proclamation*. New York: Doubleday and Co., Inc., 1963.

Harwell, Richard B. *The Confederate Reader*. New York: Longmans, Green and Company, 1957.

Katz, William Loren. *Eyewitness: The Negro in American History*. New York: Pitman and Company, 1967.

McPherson, James M. *Marching Toward Freedom: The Negro in the Civil War*. New York: Alfred A. Knopf, 1965.

Nevins, Allan. *The Ordeal of the Union*. 2 vols. New York: Charles Scribner's Sons, 1947.

Newman, Ralph G. *Lincoln for the Ages*. New York: Pyramid Books, 1960.

Sandburg, Carl. *Abraham Lincoln: The War Years*. 4 vols. New York: Harcourt, Brace & Company, 1939.

Stampp, Kenneth M. *The Peculiar Institution*. New York: Alfred A. Knopf, 1956.

Stern, Philip Van Doren (ed.) *Prologue to Sumter*. New York: Fawcett World Library, 1961.

Wiley, Bell Irwin. *Life of Johnny Reb*. Indianapolis: The Bobbs-Merrill Company, Inc., 1943.

INDEX

★☆★☆★

(Numbers in italics indicate information contained in captions.)

Abolitionists, 14, 33
Africa, slaves from, 2, 3, 5
    See also Slavery.
Agriculture, 1, 23, 35
Amendment to the Constitution, 13, 77
Anderson, Robert, 24
Andersonville. *See* Prisons.
Antietam, 36
Antislavery forces, *15*
Appomattox, 68, 69, *73*

Beauregard, P. G. T., 24
Bell, John, 19
Blacks in military, *28*, 34, 35, *43, 44, 46, 49, 50, 57, 61, 65, 71*
Blacks in the North, 4-5
    See also Blacks in military.
Blacks in the South. *See* Slavery.
Blockades, *31*, 77
Booth, John Wilkes, 69, *74*
Brady, Matthew, *28, 53*
Breckenridge, John, 19
Brooks, Preston, 14
Brown, John, 14, 18, 19, *20*
Bull Run, 24, 25
Butler, Ben, 34, *39*

Calhoun, John C., 11, 12
California, admission to Union, 12
Charleston, 35
Cities, 1
    See also individual cities.
Clay, Henry, 12
Communications, 28
Compromise of 1850, 13

Confederate States of America, 22, 27, *31*
    See also Davis, Jefferson *and* Lee, Robert E.
Constitution, Confederate, *27*
Contrabands of war, slaves as, 34
Copperheads. *See* Draft riots.
Cotton gin, 11
Crops, Southern, 1

Davis, Jefferson, 22, 27, 55, 56, 68
Declaration of Independence, 5
Douglas, Stephen A., 12, 13, 18, 19
Douglass, Frederick, *39*
Draft Law of the Confederacy, 56
Draft riots, 46, 47, *50*

Economic policies, *61*
Emancipation, 35, 36
Emancipation Proclamation, 36, *40, 43*
Everett, Edward, 54

Farragut, David, *25*
Five Forks, Battle of, 68
Food supplies, *63*
Ford Theater, 69
Fort Clark, *31*
Fort Hatteras, *31*
Fort Pillow, *65*, 57
Fort Sumter, 23, 24, 25, 27, 35
Frèmont, John C., 14, 33

Garibaldi Regiment, 77
Garrison, William Lloyd, 11
Gettysburg, 47, 54, *58*
Gettysburg Address, 54
Grant, Ulysses S., 47, *53*, 54, 55, 68, 69, *73*

ABOUT THE
AUTHOR

★☆★☆★☆ For fifteen years, William Loren Katz has taught United States history to high school students. He has served as a consultant to state departments of education and to the Smithsonian Institution. He is presently Consulting Editor for a series of picture albums on ethnic minority groups in America today and author of *Constitutional Amendments* (A First Book), both published by Franklin Watts, Inc.

His other works include the award-winning *Eyewitness: The Negro in American History* (1967); *American Majorities and Minorities* (1970); and *The Black West: A Documentary and Pictorial History* (1971). Mr. Katz is presently working on several other books to be published by Franklin Watts, Inc.: *An Album of Reconstruction; A History of Ethnic Minority Groups in America* (6 volumes); and a study of *Violence in America.* Mr. Katz lives in New York City and is currently a scholar-in-residence at Teachers College, Columbia University.